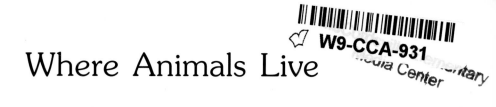

Where Animals Live

The World of Deer

Adapted from Linda Gamlin's *The Deer in the Forest*

Words by
David Saintsing

Photographs by
Oxford Scientific Films

Gareth Stevens Children's Books
MILWAUKEE

Published 7-91
10.95 E

Contents

Note: The use of a capital letter for a deer's name means that it is a specific *type* (or *species*) of deer (such as the White-tailed Deer). The use of a lower case, or small, letter for a deer's name means that it is a member of a larger *group* of deer.

Where Deer Live

Deer are among the most beautiful animals in the forest. They have large, gentle eyes, long ears, and glossy red-brown coats. They are very quiet and shy, so it is sometimes hard to spot wild deer. But you can often find their tracks in the mud or snow.

There are many different *species* of deer, and they are found in almost every country of the world. Most live in wooded areas.

Some, like the Muntjac, live in the jungles of countries like India. Others, like the Fallow or White-tailed Deer, live in the forests of cooler areas like Europe and North America. And others, like the Moose (called Elk in Europe), live in the cold lands of the far north.

Beyond the Forest ⬆

Few deer stay in the forest all the time. Often the best food is found at the edge of the woods. Here, there are lots of berries and grass.

Some deer, like these Caribou (called Reindeer in Europe), spend all of their lives out of the forest. The Caribou live on the *tundra*. They stay in herds to protect themselves from *predators*.

⬇

In South America, the Pampas Deer lives outside the forest. It hides unseen in tall grass called *pampas*.

These types of deer moved out of the forests thousands of years ago. When land is cleared for farming, other types of deer are forced out of the forests. The Red Deer of Scotland is a good example. It once lived in pine forests that are now open moors. The moors are hard on the young deer, and almost half die in their first winter.

The Forest's Changing Seasons

Winter is the hardest time of the year for deer, and many die of starvation. In *deciduous* forests, the trees shed their leaves each winter in order to grow a new crop each spring. This cycle of growth and death affects all the living things in the forest — even deer. The type and amount of food that is available to deer change with each season.

In the spring and early summer, the young leaves of trees are tender and juicy. There is a variety of plants for deer to choose from. Later in the year, deer must put on extra fat for the winter. They feast on nuts, berries, and other rich foods. By early winter, they are sleek and fat. In the winter, deer must nibble on mosses, evergreen plants, and even twigs and bark. These plants will help them survive the winter.

Being flexible about what to eat helps deer survive in the changing seasons of the deciduous forest.

Food is not all that changes with the seasons. So does the undergrowth that grows on the forest floor. Newborn deer are not strong enough to escape from predators. Like this baby Mule Deer, *fawns* hide in the undergrowth while their mothers feed. Most deer give birth in the spring and early summer because this is when the undergrowth is thickest.

The Deer's Body

Like most *mammals*, deer have a coat of fur to help keep them warm in winter. This fur is reddish-brown in most species and changes to grayish-brown in winter. The summer fur is *molted*, or shed, each year, and the winter fur grows in its place.

Each hair of the deer is hollow and filled with air. The air in all the hairs helps deer float in the water — just like a life jacket!

Deer have hard springy hooves that leave a telltale track. But their sharp senses — hearing, sight, and smell — warn deer when predators are near. Their large eyes give deer a good view all around. And their sensitive noses help them build a "picture" of smells around them.

Their long legs make deer very fast runners and high jumpers. A large deer can easily jump a fence 8 1/2 feet (2.6 m) high!

A deer's sense of smell also helps it mark off its *territory*. Deer have scent *glands* at the base of their antlers and on their hooves. This male White-tailed deer is rubbing his scent, or smell, onto a stick. The scent comes from a gland at the base of his left antler.

Deer also scrape away bare areas on the ground with their hooves. These areas have the scent of the deer, and they also mark off its territory.

Antlers

Here is a male Caribou, or Reindeer, with a huge set of antlers. Deer are the only animals in the world to have antlers. Unlike horns, antlers are made of bone. And deer drop, or "cast," their antlers once a year and grow a new set. Also, antlers grow only on the male. This is true of all deer except the Caribou. No one is really sure why this is so. But the antlers do help the female defend their young against predators.

Antlers can also be quite small, like the backward-pointing antlers of the Muntjac (above left), from Asia. But for most males, it is important to have large antlers. During breeding, males compete for females. Large antlers are good for fighting other males.

In one picture below, the male has just cast, or dropped off, his antlers. In the other, a cast antler lies on the ground. After the antlers are cast, a new, larger set begins to grow.

As the antlers grow, they are covered with a thick layer of furry skin called "velvet." This skin contains many blood vessels. They carry *nutrients* to the growing antlers.

The antlers of this Alaskan Caribou are fully grown. They are hard and will not grow any more. He therefore does not need the velvet. He has begun to get rid of it by rubbing it off on trees and bushes.

Food and Digestion

Deer eat many kinds of food: nuts, fruit, mushrooms, twigs, and even tree bark. But it is grass, leaves, and buds that make up most of their diet. Deer that like grass more than anything else are called *grazers* (above). Deer that prefer leaves are called *browsers* (below).

Deer will go to great lengths to get their food. Moose often wade into a lake to get at water plants, as this one is doing.

Plants have something called cellulose in them. Most mammals cannot *digest* cellulose. But deer have *bacteria* in their stomachs which can break down cellulose. Once the bacteria break cellulose down, the deer can absorb it and use it to fatten up. The deer's waste is passed out in droppings like those of a rabbit.

Life with the Herd

Some species of deer live in large groups called herds. Staying in a herd helps deer defend themselves against predators. Herds are especially important for females and their young. Because of their size and strength, males often live alone for part of the year.

In winter, being in a herd helps deer be sure to find food. The many deer hooves pound the ground. This helps trample away the snow and clear a space where the deer can feed on the grass. This space is called a "yard."

Even deer that usually live alone may come together in herds.

Fighting for a Mate

Most deer breed in September, October, or November. In late summer, the antlers finish growing, and the male rubs off the velvet on bushes or tree trunks. This makes marks on the trees which show the deer's territory.

Each male deer also makes a lot of noise. Some, like this Wapiti stag, "bugle." Others grunt, bellow, whistle, or even bark like dogs!

A male deer's scent also marks its territory. All
this noise and smell may keep other males out.
But sometimes males fight over the right to
mate with a female. In most species, the
strongest males mate with more than one
female. You can see that these Wapiti (below)
have smaller antlers than the older Wapiti on
page 20. This means that they have less chance
of mating. And they might not be grown
enough to mate until they are six or seven years
old.

Giving Birth

Most deer give birth to one fawn. But some, like this Red Deer, have twins. Females give birth in late spring. This is when there is lots of undergrowth for the fawn to hide in.

Most fawns stay still in their hiding places during the first week or two. The mothers feed alone and return to nurse their young two or three times a day. This Moose (below) will go on giving her young milk for six months or more.

A young deer usually stays with its mother for one year, until she is getting ready to have another fawn. Fawns are usually spotted to give them *camouflage*. This coat is kept for several months before the adult fur grows in.

Predators and Other Dangers

In remote parts of North America, adult deer can fall *prey* to Mountain Lions (above), eagles, wolves, and Grizzly Bears. In places like Yellowstone National Park, they still kill many deer. But elsewhere, many of these predators have been killed by humans, and they are rare in places where people live.

Black Bears do not kill deer. But they will feed on any dead ones that they find, as this one is doing.

Deer fawns face many dangers as they lie in the underbrush. Their main predators are foxes, dogs, and coyotes.

Humans also kill deer, and millions of deer are shot each year by hunters for food or sport. Many others are killed as they cross roads. Some are even poisoned by the *pesticides* we put on our crops. Winter is also a cause of death among deer. Snow, ice, and the lack of food combine to kill many deer.

25

Deer and Humans

Humans have always taken good care of deer so that they can continue to hunt them. People have even moved deer from one part of the world to another. For example, ancestors of these Fallow Deer (above) were shipped from France to Britain, and from Britain to North America.

Prehistoric cave paintings in France show that people have been hunting deer for 40,000 years.

Sometimes deer are brought into an area not for hunting, but just so people can enjoy watching them in parks.

But not everyone loves deer! Many of our trees and plants need special protection from hungry deer.

The Forest by Night and Day

Early mornings just before dawn (above) or evenings are the best times for deer to feed. They are safer from predators at these times. But there is just enough light to find food. Also, deer are safer from predators after dark.

Many animals share the night with deer. Foxes (above right) and raccoons feed on both live prey and fruit.

Night is also busy for smaller forest animals. Mice (right), shrews, and voles feed at night. And they are preyed upon by owls and weasels.

As the sun rises, most of these animals disappear from sight. The only mammals that really like the daylight are the squirrels. Squirrels feed mostly on nuts, a favorite of most animals in the forest. Deer eat nuts too, but they also eat food that is not a favorite of other animals. Leaves and grass are hard to digest. But deer have a way of digesting them. So the deer have one food source that is not used by many other animals.

Life in the Forest

Deer eat only plants. And they once provided food to meat-eaters, such as the wolf and bear, so they were a major link in the food chain below. But today this food chain is much simpler, because now deer are killed mainly by human hunters.

Food Chain

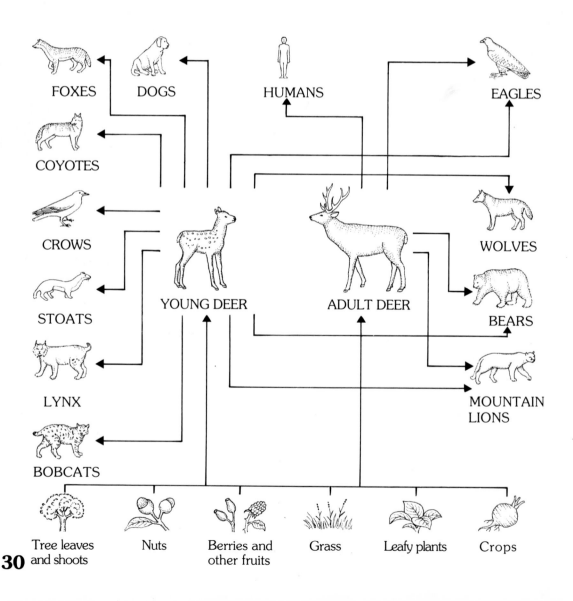

FOXES DOGS HUMANS EAGLES

COYOTES

CROWS YOUNG DEER ADULT DEER WOLVES

STOATS

LYNX BEARS

BOBCATS MOUNTAIN LIONS

Tree leaves and shoots Nuts Berries and other fruits Grass Leafy plants Crops

Like these Red Deer in Scotland, deer survive by adapting to many changes. Some of these changes are in the seasons. Others are in their food supply. Deer have also survived by looking out for predators. Now the predator they must watch out for is the one with a gun.

Humans affect deer in many ways. We affect their numbers by hunting and replacing them. We affect their food by felling forests. Chopping down forests is usually bad for deer. To ensure their survival, we must make sure there are forests for deer to live in.

Index and New Words About Deer

These new words about deer appear in the text on the pages shown after each definition. Each new word first appears in the text in *italics*, just as it appears here.

Reading level analysis: SPACHE 2.4, FRY 2, FLESCH 94 (very easy). RAYGOR 3, FOG 4, SMOG 3

Library of Congress Cataloging-in-Publication Data

Saintsing, David and Gamlin, Linda.
The world of deer.

(Where animals live)
"Adapted from Linda Gamlin's The deer in the forest."
Includes index.
Summary: Text and photographs describe the lives of deer, including their feeding, breeding, and defense behavior.
1. Deer—Juvenile literature. [1. Deer] I. Gamlin, Linda. The deer in the forest. II. Oxford Scientific Films. III. Title. IV. Series.
QL737.U55S225   1988   599.73'57   87-6539
ISBN 1-55532-327-8
ISBN 1-55532-302-2 (lib. bdg.)

North American edition first published in 1988 by Gareth Stevens Children's Books, 1555 North RiverCenter Drive, Suite 201, Milwaukee, Wisconsin 53212, USA. U.S. edition, this format, copyright © 1988 by Belitha Press Ltd. Text copyright © 1988 by Gareth Stevens, Inc. All rights reserved. No part of this book may be reproduced in any form or by any means without permission in writing from Gareth Stevens, Inc. First conceived, designed, and produced by Belitha Press Ltd., London, as **The Deer in the Forest**, with an original text copyright by Oxford Scientific Films. Format copyright by Belitha Press Ltd. Series Editor: Mark J. Sachner. Art Director: Treld Bicknell. Design: Naomi Games. Cover Design: Gary Moseley. Line Drawings: Lorna Turpin. Scientific Consultants: Gwynne Vevers and David Saintsing.

The publishers wish to thank the following for permission to reproduce copyrighted photographs: **Oxford Scientific Films Ltd.** for p. 2 (S. Meyers); pp. 3, 4 above, 12 below, 18, 20 top right, 22 above, 31, and back cover (Terry Heathcote); p. 4 below (Richard Barnell); pp. 5, 11 top right, and 17 below (Barrie E. Watts); p. 6 (Raymond Blythe); p. 7 (Sean Morris); pp. 8, 12 above, 13, 24, and front cover (Leonard Lee Rue III/Animals Animals); p. 9 (Stuffer Productions Ltd.); pp. 10 above, 20 above left, and 20 below (Ray Richardson); pp. 15, and 16 below (David C. Fritts); pp. 11 top left, 14 top left, top right, and below left (Press-Tige Pictures); pp. 11 below, 16 above, 21, and 25 (Stan Osolinkski); pp. 14 below right and 17 above (Stephen Fuller); p. 19 (Mark Newman); p. 22 below (Harry Engels); p. 23 (Breck P. Kent); p. 26 (David and Sue Cayless); p. 27 below (Alastair Shay); pp. 28 and 29 above (David Cayless); p. 29 below (David Houghton); Bruce Coleman Ltd. for title page (Hans Reinhard).

Printed in the United States of America.
3 4 5 6 7 8 9 96 95 94 93 92 91
For a free color catalog describing Gareth Stevens' list of high-quality children's books, call 1-800-341-3569 (USA) or 1-800-461-9120 (Canada).